BOY SCOUTS OF AMERICA
MERIT BADGE SERIES

SCULPTURE

"Enhancing our youths' competitive edge through merit badges"

BOY SCOUTS OF AMERICA®

Requirements

1. Explain to your counselor the precautions that must be followed for the safe use and operation of a sculptor's tools, equipment, and other materials.

2. Do TWO of the following:

    a. Model in clay a life-size human head. Then sculpt in modeling clay, carve in wood or plaster, or use 3D modeling software to make a small-scale model of an animal or person. Explain to your counselor the method and tools you used to sculpt the figure.

    b. Make a plaster mold of a fruit or vegetable. In this mold, make a copy of the fruit or vegetable. Explain to your counselor the method and tools you used to make the copy.

    c. With your parent's permission and your counselor's approval, visit a museum, art exhibit, art gallery, artists' co-op, or artist's studio. After your visit, share with your counselor what you have learned. Discuss the importance of visual arts and how it strengthens social tolerance and helps stimulate cultural, intellectual, and personal development.

3. Find out about career opportunities in sculpture. Pick one and find out the education, training, and experience required for this profession. Discuss this with your counselor, and explain why this profession might interest you.

35947
ISBN 978-0-8395-3322-1
©2019 Boy Scouts of America
2019 Printing

Contents

About Sculpting	5
Sculpting Basics	13
Modeling a Head	22
Making a Mask	27
Plaster Casting	33
Carving in Wood	39
Carving in Soapstone	43
Experimenting With Sculpture	47
Art Spaces and Places	53
Careers in Sculpture	58
Sculpture Resources	61

Robert Indiana's *LOVE* sculpture

SCULPTURE 3

Evening Sun (left) and *Noonday Sun (right),* both by Jean Woodham

About Sculpting

Our world and the objects in it, such as humans, trees, and buildings, have three dimensions: length, width, and depth. Sculpture is an art form that allows you to express what you see and feel by using these three dimensions when shaping materials such as clay and wood.

The art of sculpture is part of the earliest human history. Using bones and soft stone, early humans carved the shapes of animals and people. As civilization developed, so did ideas about the uses and forms of sculpture. Some forms might be realistic representations, while others might be abstract forms invented by the artist. These *abstractions,* with little or no realistic form, express the artist's emotions or attitude.

The material an artist uses often dictates a sculpture's form. For example, hard stone might express heavy solid shapes. Soft stone lends itself to more intricate or delicate shapes. Metal can be cast at high temperatures or made into sheets and rods, which may be used to create solid or airy forms. Clay, which is soft, can be easily shaped and detailed. The artist may follow the wood grain to carve the shape of a sculpture.

Argus, **by Jean Woodham**

Sculpture can be almost anything that is three-dimensional: a statue, a mobile, a monument, or a portrait.

About Sculpting

Sculptors have almost no size limitations on their creations. They may make sculpture as small as a finger. Some are as large as a mountain, such as the one carved with drills and dynamite in Mount Rushmore in South Dakota. Starting in 1927, sculptor Gutzon Borglum, his crew, and his son patiently worked on Mount Rushmore for more than 14 years to sculpt the faces of four U.S. presidents—George Washington, Thomas Jefferson, Abraham Lincoln, and Theodore Roosevelt.

Another mountain carving in South Dakota, only 17 miles from Mount Rushmore, is of Oglala Sioux chief Crazy Horse riding a horse. Sculptor Korczak Ziolkowski, who had worked briefly on the Mount Rushmore sculpture in 1939 as Borglum's assistant, started the Crazy Horse Memorial in 1948.

Ziolkowski and his helpers used explosives, jackhammers, and torches to work on the 563-foot-tall, 641-foot-long statue in the mountain. Crazy Horse's face is as tall as a nine-story building, and the horse's face stands 22 stories high. During the work, Ziolkowski also carved a 3,000-pound statue of frontiersman Wild Bill Hickok and a 7-ton statue of Teton Sioux chief Sitting Bull from the granite he had blasted from the mountain. He also built his own tomb near the statue of Crazy Horse.

Korczak Ziolkowski

Mount Rushmore

ABOUT SCULPTING

Ziolkowski worked on the mountain project until his death at age 74 in 1982. His wife and seven sons and daughters have continued to carve the Crazy Horse Memorial.

Work on Korczak Ziolkowski's mountain carving that depicts Oglala Sioux chief Crazy Horse continues today. The statue in the foreground *(above)* shows what the completed carving will look like. The overhead view *(right)* shows the massive scale of the project.

It is interesting to learn about the ideas or themes sculptors think about when they create their art. Often, sculptors gain reputations for a particular style, material, or subject matter. Frederick Hart, Louise Nevelson, and David Smith are among those who had their own unique way of sculpting and are admired for their creativity and dedication.

SCULPTURE 7

ABOUT SCULPTING

Frederick Hart

American sculptor Frederick Hart (1943–1999) is best known for his monumental works. *The Creation Sculptures* on the west facade of the Washington National Cathedral, Washington, D.C., were begun in 1972 and dedicated in 1990. Recognized by many art authorities as the most important religious sculptures in an architectural setting in the 20th century, they consist of three life-size statues—*Adam, St. Peter,* and *St. Paul*—and three relief panels—*Creation of Night, Creation of Day,* and *Ex Nihilo* ("Out of Nothing")—all carved from Indiana limestone.

Three Soldiers© 1984, Hart & VVMF

Frederick Hart's most visited monument is the heroic *Three Soldiers,* a bronze statue at the Vietnam Veterans Memorial in Washington, D.C. It was dedicated by President Ronald Reagan in 1984.

In 1997, Hart presented *The Cross of the Millennium* to Pope John Paul II, who called it "a profound theological statement for our day." The masterpiece utilized Hart's patented casting technique of embedding one clear acrylic sculpture within another.

SCULPTURE

===== ABOUT SCULPTING

The artistic and historic importance of *The Creation Sculptures, Three Soldiers,* and *The Cross of the Millennium* are discussed in *Masters of American Sculpture,* by Dr. Donald Martin Reynolds, noted authority on public monuments in the United States.

Frederick Hart believed in creating sculptures that deeply move people to revere and reflect upon the greatness, the splendor, and the beauty of nature, of God, and of humankind.

Louise Nevelson*

Louise Nevelson (1899–1988) emigrated from Ukraine to the United States with her family and grew up in Rockland, Maine. Although she lived in cold climates, she always disliked the cold. She remembered her classrooms as cold. The only room in school where she felt warm was the art room. She said, "It had nothing to do with the temperature. It had something to do with my generating heat." She was referring to the passion, enjoyment, and enthusiasm she had for her work.

Nevelson struggled to make a living as a sculptor in New York City. It took her a long time to achieve a reputation, because she held fast to her independence. Nevelson liked to dress with style, and people assumed that a woman who did not wear the 1940s artist's "uniform" of a beret and old clothes could not be dedicated, serious, or talented.

Louise Nevelson's *Transparent Horizon* (1975), on the campus of Massachusetts Institute of Technology in Cambridge, Massachusetts

*Some of the information for the biography of Louise Nevelson was drawn from the "Oral History Interview With Louise Nevelson," by Arnald Glimcher, Smithsonian Archives of American Art, 1972.

SCULPTURE 9

About Sculpting

From early childhood, Nevelson knew that she had to be an artist. She decided to become a sculptor because, as she said, "I don't want color to help me."

Rain Garden II (1977), a sculptural wall by Louise Nevelson

Although Nevelson worked in materials such as Plexiglas, metal, and plastic, wood was her favorite material. Her best-known sculptures—"sculptural walls"—began as shallow boxes or trays filled with wooden objects she found in the streets or in antiques shops. These pieces of wood—knobs, chair slats, wheels, broken boards with nails in them—became interesting abstract forms as she assembled them in her boxes.

She began to stack the boxes vertically so they resembled walls. They had height and width but fairly shallow depth. She usually painted these "walls" black, giving the viewer the impression of a three-dimensional abstract painting.

David Smith

David Smith (1906–1965) was born in Decatur, Indiana. Smith explored the artistic and sculptural uses of welded metal. Metalwork may have been in his blood, as one of his ancestors had been a blacksmith. During his lifetime, many regarded Smith as one of the most inventive and productive American sculptors.

ABOUT SCULPTING

For most of his career, Smith focused on iron, which, unlike marble or bronze, was not considered an "artistic" material. Smith's sculptures often featured objects and tools that had been thrown away. For example, using materials he found in five abandoned factories in Italy, Smith in one month made 27 sculptures.

Smith sometimes painted his abstract sculpture in bright colors. He also worked in stainless steel, polishing his stainless steel sculptures so they would take on the colors of the sky. The blunt lines and sense of enduring strength seen in Smith's work has prompted many scholars to view his work as an expression of industrial power.

Smith was a fast worker. In the last 13 years of his life, he created more than 400 pieces.

David Smith's *The Banquet* (1951), at the estate of John D. Rockefeller in Sleepy Hollow, New York

Sculpting Basics

Sculpting is similar to painting or drawing a picture, because it is a means of expressing what you see or feel. But unlike a picture, a sculpture is a three-dimensional form based on an arrangement of surfaces and spaces.

Visualizing Movement

If you want to be a sculptor, you should study the form and movement of everything around you. Watch animals moving or people walking, dancing, or running. What in their shapes conveys the idea of movement or action? Observe the way balance shifts when a figure stands, then runs. Visualize the kind of movement you want your sculpture to express before you begin making the piece.

One way of visualizing action is to do *gesture drawings*. These are quick sketches that are not meant to show exactly what the subject looks like but to show what it is doing. Use a pen, brush, or felt-tip pen to make your drawing. Watch a person or animal in action and then draw it quickly—in a few seconds. You cannot possibly put in all the details, so look instead for the lines that show action.

SCULPTING BASICS

For centuries, artists have used materials such as clay, stone, wood, and metal to model, carve, or cast sculpture. Modern materials such as plastics and aerated concrete, and newer techniques such as welding and brazing, have expanded the possibilities for artistic expression.

Looking at Sculpture

Because it is three-dimensional, sculpture usually is designed to be observed from all sides, with each side as important as another. When making a sculpture, you should decide how you want your work to look from each angle, keeping in mind that certain factors such as light as well as positive and negative space change the sculpture's appearance.

Light

Simple objects become sculptural if you look at them in different ways. For example, try placing an egg on a piece of white paper. It still looks like an egg. Now use a flashlight or an ordinary lamp to shine light on the egg from various angles. The light and shadow play on the shape and volume of the egg and it now becomes a piece of art. Light reveals form in sculpture the way shading with a pencil reveals form in a drawing.

Use more complex objects—including your face—to see how shining a light on them from different angles changes their appearance.

Positive and Negative Space

Besides light, there are two other important factors involved in designing a piece of sculpture: *positive space* and *negative space*. The egg, for example, is called the positive space and the space around the egg (where the egg isn't) is called the negative space.

Look at a chair to see the positive and negative spaces. While the chair is solid (positive space), you may notice negative space within the solid form. You will see that the space between the back of the chair and the seat has a shape and so does the space between the four legs. The negative space within the chair's form gives an impression of lightness. On the other hand, if you look at a dense sculpture, such as a figure of a hippopotamus, you will see a compact shape. The negative space surrounds the hippo, giving an impression of heaviness.

Sculpting Basics

As its negative space shifts, a mobile becomes a moving sculpture.

Negative space may play just as important a role in the overall impact of a sculpture as positive space. In David Smith's work, for example, negative space takes on its own form and becomes a part of the piece. If you visit art museums, you may have seen works by Alexander Calder, who is known as the inventor of the mobile as an art form. He made negative space an even more important element of sculpture because his mobiles constantly create new negative space as their parts move.

Subtractive and Additive Techniques

Artists use *subtractive techniques* or *additive techniques* to create sculpture. In subtractive sculpting, as in wood or stone carving, material is removed until the form is revealed. In additive sculpture, as in modeling with clay, material is added to create the finished form.

American sculptor Jo Davidson (1883–1952) used the additive technique to create portrait heads of such notables as Franklin D. Roosevelt and Albert Einstein. Davidson once said: "To model, you start with nothing and add on until you have something. To carve, you start with too much and by cutting away with a knife, chisel, or other implement, you cut it down to what you want to express."

This bust of Gen. Omar Bradley (1893–1981) appears on display at the national office of the Boy Scouts of America in Irving, Texas.

16   SCULPTURE

SCULPTING BASICS

Materials

There is quite a variety of materials you can use to make sculptures. Choose a material based on the properties of the material and the type of sculpture you plan to make.

Clay probably is the oldest sculptural material. There are several types of clay you can use. **Terra-cotta,** which has been used since prehistoric times, is perhaps the best. After allowing a clay piece to dry, you fire it in a *kiln,* a very hot oven in which clay objects are placed to permanently harden them.

Modeling clay (Plasteline or Plastalina) is a soft, oily, synthetic clay that does not harden and can be used to make a mold of a sculpture.

Sculpey, a synthetic clay, is a good choice for small projects. It is soft and hardens only when placed in an oven. There also are self-hardening clays that must be kept wet until a project is finished.

Plaster of paris is an inexpensive, quick-hardening paste. It may be cast into blocks and then carved with a *rasp,* a coarse file with cutting points that is used for scraping or smoothing wood or metal.

Plaster cloth is an open-weave cloth, such as gauze, with plaster of paris embedded in the fabric. When moistened, it can be formed or wrapped to almost any shape. Plaster cloth dries in about 15 minutes.

Remember to wash your hands with soap and water after using clay, modeling clay, Sculpey, plaster of paris, or plaster cloth.

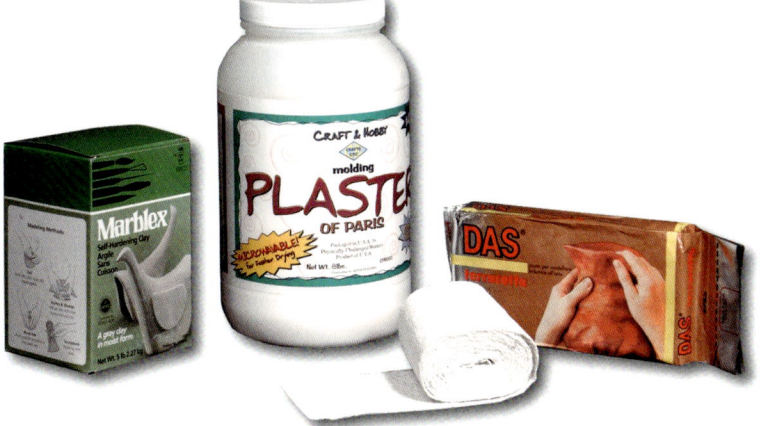

When using any sculpting materials, be sure to follow the manufacturer's instructions.

SCULPTURE 17

SCULPTING BASICS

Tools

Fingers probably are the most useful tools for working with soft clays. You can use a *loop tool,* a wooden tool with a metal loop on the end, to trim away excess clay. If you are working with soapstone (a soft stone), you will need a rasp and a *riffler,* a metal tool similar to a rasp with fine, small cutting points on one or both ends.

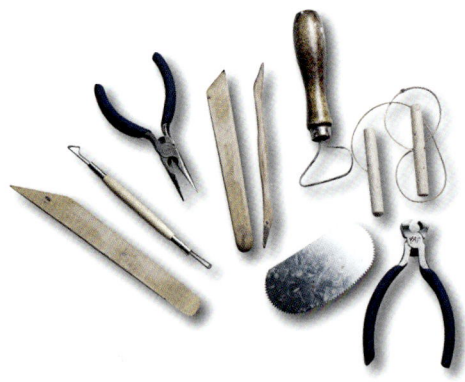

These commercial tools come in handy for the artist working with clay.

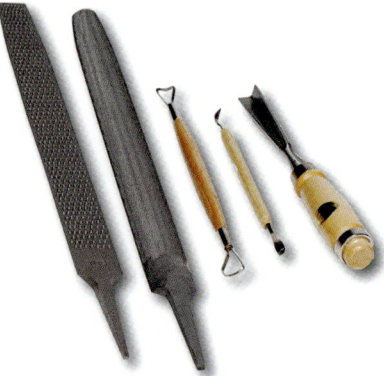

Use wood-carving tools, such as rasps, files, gouges, chisels, and V-tools, with great care.

Whenever you see this icon, there will be safety information that goes with it.

Even though soapstone is quite soft, it still requires a lot of effort to carve a form. It is best to keep your design simple. For carving wood, you will usually need *gouges* (handheld tools with curved cutting edges) or regular *chisels,* which are sharp-edged metal tools that you can use to cut away and shape the material.

Safety

Be careful that you use tools safely. When using knives and chisels to make wood sculptures, always carve and cut away from your body. Pay attention to the placement of your fingers on the material. Your counselor might advise that you wear protective gloves. And take your time. When carving and chipping wood, it's a good idea to wear protective goggles, especially if you will be using hand tools or power tools.

18   SCULPTURE

> Lightweight paper "dust masks" are not designed as protection against toxic dust and vapors. Use a respiratory mask.

If you ever work with sanding machines or anything else that will produce dust particles, wear a protective respiratory mask. It is also a good idea to wear one when working with clay. If you use electrical equipment, such as a grinder, do not wear loose-fitting clothes.

When working with clay, glazes, paints, or other materials that can produce toxic dust or vapors, wear a toxic dust respiratory mask approved by the National Institute for Occupational Safety and Health (NIOSH), disposable gloves, and work clothing made of materials that will not collect dust. Separate these clothes from other laundry and wash them weekly.

Avoid food areas when working on any project, and do not eat or drink in the work areas. If you work clay with bare hands, wash your hands thoroughly with soap and water. If you find it very time consuming to get your hands clean after working with clay, you might want to try an art soap specifically designed to wash off clay.

It is best to use premixed clay to avoid exposure to large quantities of clay dust. Be careful when firing clay in a kiln. If it is burned or scorched, the clay can emit dangerous fumes. Although you can fire polymer (synthetic) clays such as Sculpey in an ordinary kitchen oven at temperatures from 250 to 275 degrees, you should still take precautions. Get the advice of your instructor before attempting to fire polymer clays.

If you need to use an oven for your project, do so only under the direct supervision of a responsible adult.

Use a kiln only under the direct supervision of a qualified adult instructor who is familiar with its operation. Be sure the area is well-ventilated, with an adequate exhaust system. If you look into a kiln when it is firing, be sure to wear infrared goggles approved by the American National Standards Institute (ANSI), or use a handheld welding shield with a shade number of 1.7 to 3.0.

SCULPTING BASICS

Armatures

To model a life-size head or small-scale animal or person, you might need an *armature*, a framework that gives inner support to a soft material such as clay. You can make one by using a piece of threaded pipe and a flange screwed to a wood base. The materials can be purchased at a building-supply store.

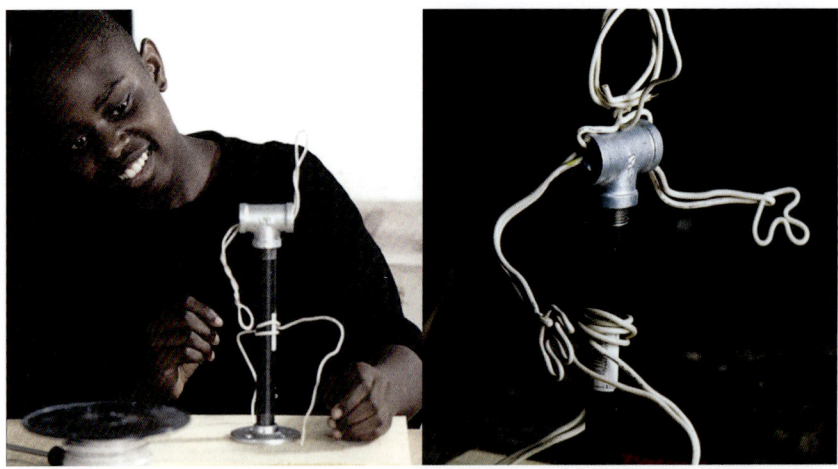

Making an armature will help give your model inner support as you work on it.

To build a complex armature, you will need a threaded metal pipe or PVC pipe, 6 to 12 inches long and ½ to 1 inch in diameter, and a flange for the pipe to screw or fit into. Screw the flange into the center of an 8-inch-square board. Screw one end of the pipe into the flange and the other end into a T-shaped pipe. To make a life-size head, attach an aluminum wire (6 gauge works well) to the top of the T-shaped pipe and shape it like a circle. For arms, thread the wire through the T-shaped pipe; for legs, wrap wire around the lower area of the pipe.

A piece of 2-by-2-inch or 2-by-4-inch wood that is at least 12 inches long also will work in place of the threaded pipe. Use an 8-by-8-inch or 10-by-10-inch piece of plywood or a board of similar size for the base. Drill a hole in the center of the base so that you can use a large wood screw to fasten the 12-inch piece of wood upright to the base. This will give you an armature to mold your sculpting material around when shaping a head or figure.

SCULPTING BASICS

Ceramic Sculpture

One of the earliest ways people used clay was to make ceramic pottery. Artists make sculpture with the same basic methods today, although the clay they use might be different from that used to make pottery.

A clay body is a combination of clays and minerals blended together for a specific ceramic purpose. There are three major types of clay bodies: earthenware, stoneware, and porcelain.

Earthenware usually is full of impurities that give the clay different color ranges and cause it to mature (harden) at low temperatures. Because the clay does not completely solidify into a watertight state, sculptors may apply glaze inside and out. Terra-cotta is a type of earthenware.

Stoneware fires at a higher temperature, which leaves the surface hard and nonporous. It is usually opaque (not transparent), but when it is shaped to be very thin, it may let some light through. Sculptors often combine several clays with grog or sand to make a stoneware clay body.

Porcelain, made from a pure clay fused by intense heat, has a smooth, white surface. Some porcelain objects are known as whiteware, including china and plumbing fixtures such as toilets and sinks.

> Grog, which is ground-up unglazed fired clay, is usually added to the clay to make it more porous and easier to form into irregular shapes.

SCULPTURE 21

Modeling a Head

One of the best ways to get a feel for modeling is to experiment by molding the material into different shapes. After doing this, you might want to try shaping clay into a head. There is no need to try for perfection—the head does not have to look like anyone you know. The purpose of this requirement is simply to introduce you to the basics of sculpting.

Using Terra-Cotta

When using terra-cotta, you will need an armature on which to model your clay head. You must place something over the upright pipe of the armature to make the head hollow. Try using a ball of newspaper to shape the head. Then slip a paper bag over the newspaper and twist the bottom around the pipe.

To make the head, start by covering the armature with small bits of clay. Keep adding clay until the surface is a half inch thick. A tight bond between bits of clay is important. The clay shrinks as it dries and will crack at weak joints. If the terra-cotta seems to dry too much while you are working with it, dampen the clay with a wet sponge or cloth. If you cannot finish the head in one session, cover it with a damp cloth and plastic until you work on it again.

You can start making facial features on the head by pressing your thumbs into the clay to indicate where the eyes should be. Place a long piece of rolled clay down the middle of the face to set up the profile. Push the clay around to shape the nose, lips, and chin. Draw in lines for the eyebrows and lips. Use a metal loop tool to gouge out eye sockets. Keep adding clay and massaging it to form the forehead, brow, and cheeks. Work around the head, building up the back of the head, too. Roll out two ovals for ears and place them on the sides of the head between the brow and nose tip. Add more clay for hair. Use your fingers to blend and smooth the clay, and use pointed tools to carve details.

> As you study real people and work on the full-size head, you probably will realize that a face is not symmetrical; that is, the left and right sides do not match exactly.

MODELING A HEAD

If you plan to fire the head in a kiln, you must first remove the armature. Let the terra-cotta become "leather dry" before you try to pull out the paper. Then take a very thin wire about 16 inches long and carefully slice the head in two, behind the ears. Remove the armature. Scratch the edges of the two parts where they will touch when you rejoin them. This step helps the clay parts "grab" each other. Make some *slip* (clay mixed with water to the consistency of cream) and paste it on the scratched surfaces. Wiggle the pieces a little to create suction. Then blend some clay to get rid of the seam. Let the head dry on a pillow.

> Terra-cotta must be completely dry before being fired in a kiln. The drying could take several days, depending on the size of the head. Any moisture in the sculpture will make it explode during firing. Ask your instructor to check the head for dryness. One way to tell is to hold the sculpture to your cheek. If it feels cold, it still has moisture in it and is not safe to fire.

Kiln Caution

Firing clay requires technical knowledge and can be dangerous. For your sculpture project, leave the firing to a qualified instructor.

SCULPTURE 23

MODELING A HEAD

You will need an armature for making a full-size human head using modeling clay.

Using Modeling Clay

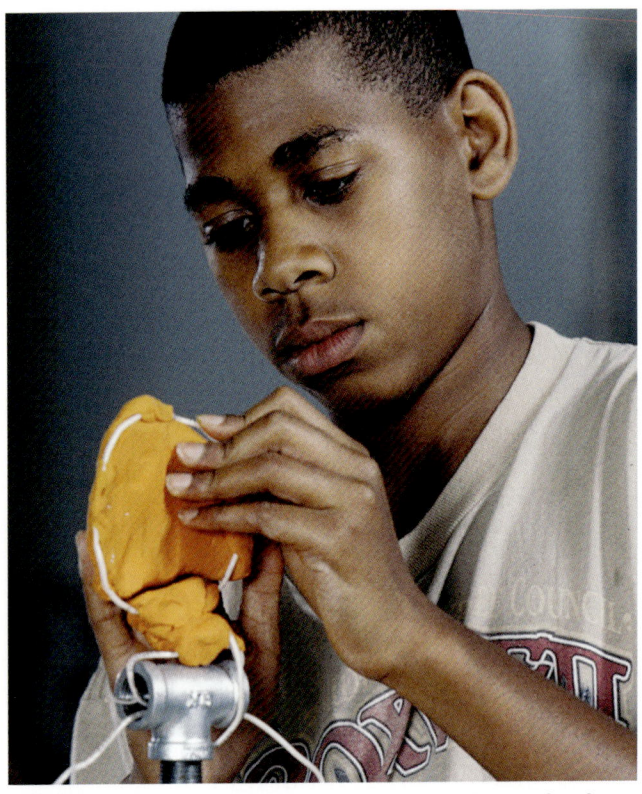

If you plan to use modeling clay for making your life-size head, you will need to model the head on an armature. Modeling clay will not dry completely while you work, but you will need to keep it moist. Build your piece gradually by adding small pieces of clay to the armature. You will probably need more than one session to finish the head, so cover it tightly with plastic to keep it from drying out when you are not working on it. The sculpture is finished when it looks the way you want it to look.

Using Plaster Cloth

You can use plaster cloth to model a head. You might form the shape of the head with the plaster cloth and then add plaster of paris to finish the piece. It is up to you whether to use an armature. If you do use an armature, it will become a permanent part of the piece, because you will not be able to remove it.

Here is what you will need.

☐ Newspapers, garbage bags, or plastic sheeting

☐ Roll of plaster cloth

☐ Large bowl of warm water

☐ Scissors

Step 1—Cover your work surface with newspaper, garbage bags, or plastic. Dip the roll of fabric in water to thoroughly wet the plaster.

Step 2—Build the head over a form on the armature, as described in the section on making a terra-cotta head. Wrap at least two layers over the form.

Step 3—Now begin adding features by using more plaster cloth.

Step 4—Give the plaster cloth enough time to set slightly so that the face does not slump.

With a little practice, you will learn how fast to go. The plaster will need to dry for about two hours.

Making a Mask

Many cultures have used masks for religious purposes and to express their emotions in the presence of nature's power. In ancient Greece, actors often wore masks when performing plays. Modern theatrical performances sometimes still use masks.

To get started making your own mask, decide what character or animal you will portray and then gather the following supplies.

- ☐ Large garbage bags or plastic sheeting to cover the work surface
- ☐ Materials for an armature (A simple, plastic Halloween mask will do.)
- ☐ Modeling clay
- ☐ Newspaper
- ☐ Scissors
- ☐ Large bowl of water
- ☐ Paintbrush (½ to 1 inch wide)
- ☐ White glue
- ☐ Acrylic paints
- ☐ Assorted small paintbrushes
- ☐ Shellac or clear acrylic coating (optional)
- ☐ Respiratory mask (if using shellac or acrylic coating)

Because making a mask can be messy, first protect your work surface with plastic sheeting or a large garbage bag.

SCULPTURE 27

Making a Mask

Step 1—Using modeling clay, model the face on an armature. Because this is a mask, you should model the face only to the ears.

Step 2—Cut or tear the newspaper into strips about 4 inches long and 1 inch wide. Soak them in water for several hours.

Step 3—Carefully apply the wet newspaper strips around all parts of the modeling clay face. Use a brush to tamp the strips down firmly in all corners.

= Making a Mask

Step 4—Fit small pieces of newspaper tightly around corners of nose, mouth, and eyes.

Step 5—Soak more strips of newspaper at least four hours, then crumple them in water until thoroughly pliable.

Step 6—While the newspaper is soaking, coat the newspaper layer you have already placed on the mask with white glue, applying it smoothly with your fingers. You may want to thin the glue with water to make it easier to spread.

Step 7—Add the wet paper, strip by strip. Tamp down, using a brush to push the strips into close contact with the glue-covered newspaper. Allow no wrinkles or air bubbles.

Step 8—Coat the overlapped paper with white glue and add a final layer of wet newspaper.

SCULPTURE

MAKING A MASK

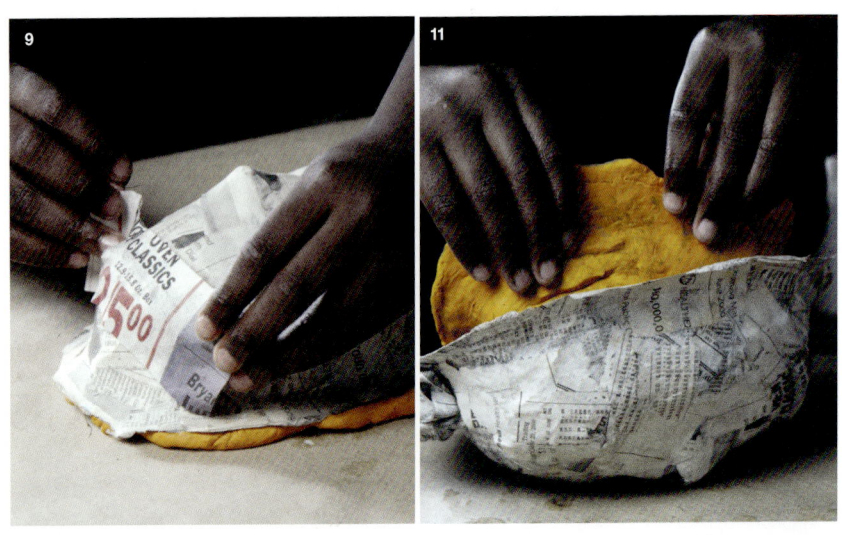

Step 9—Reinforce the top of the mask, the chin, and the jaw with an extra strip of newspaper to prevent sagging.

Step 10—Let the mask dry for several hours.

Step 11—Pull out the modeling clay mold from inside the paper mask.

Step 12—Outside or in a well-ventilated space, decorate the face with acrylic paints.

To help preserve the paint and the mask, you can spray or paint it with shellac or a clear acrylic coating. This is best done outdoors, in an open and well-ventilated area.

===================== MAKING A MASK

 When using shellac, go outside to an open area, or wear a respiratory mask. Shellac is harmful if it is inhaled.

SCULPTURE

= Plaster Casting

Plaster Casting

A copy of an object made by pouring plaster of paris into a mold is known as a *plaster cast*. Bananas and pears are the easiest to mold because both have few indentations that would make the mold more difficult to separate, and both have easily identifiable shapes.

In addition to the fruit or vegetable, you will need the following materials.

☐ Knife or box cutter

☐ Cardboard half-gallon milk container

☐ Small piece of modeling clay

☐ Petroleum jelly (or lubricating oil such as WD-40)

☐ Large plastic container

☐ Large metal spoon

☐ Plaster of paris

☐ Duct tape

☐ String or rubber bands

☐ Rasp

☐ Acrylic paints

☐ Assorted small paintbrushes

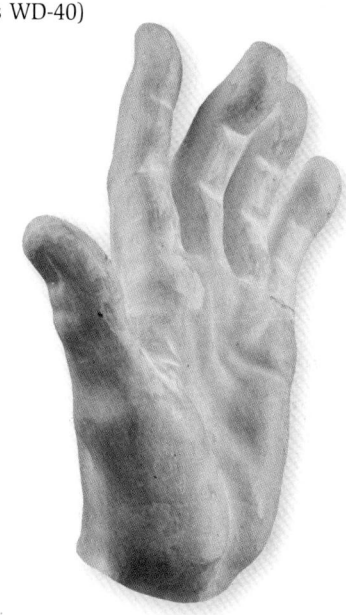

If you are feeling adventurous, try making a plaster cast of your hand. You will have fun with such a lifelike replica of the real thing.

SCULPTURE 33

Plaster Casting

Step 1—Cut the cardboard milk container into equal halves.

Step 2—Place a small piece of modeling clay inside, on the base of the container, to balance your fruit or vegetable. (For a banana, you may need two pieces.) Use enough clay so that the fruit rests about an inch or so off the bottom. Coat the fruit with a thin layer of petroleum jelly or a lubricating oil such as WD-40.

Step 3—Pour into a large plastic container enough water to fill half of the bottom part of the milk container. Sprinkle in the plaster until it starts to float on the surface. Wait a few minutes for it to settle and then stir gently to get rid of trapped air bubbles.

34   SCULPTURE

PLASTER CASTING

Step 4—Add more plaster as needed, until the mixture has the consistency of heavy cream.

Step 5—Pour the plaster around the fruit until it reaches the middle of the fruit. Work fast because the plaster sets quickly.

Step 6—Let the plaster harden.

Step 7—Coat the top of the dried plaster with a thin layer of petroleum jelly.

Step 8—Tape the two halves of the container together with duct tape.

Step 9—Now mix another batch of plaster and pour it over the top of the fruit to fill the rest of the container.

Step 10—Allow the plaster to harden overnight.

SCULPTURE   35

Plaster Casting

Step 11—Tear open the container, remove the tape, and gently separate the two halves. Remove the fruit.

Step 12—Pop out the modeling clay piece and allow the halves to thoroughly dry. This might take several days. (When dry, the plaster will not be cold to the touch.)

Step 13—You can now cast your own plaster fruit or vegetable. Coat the inside of the mold with a thin layer of petroleum jelly.

Step 14—Secure the two halves of the mold with string or rubber bands.

Step 15—Mix up enough plaster to fill the mold. Turn the mold upside down and slowly pour the plaster through the hole left by the modeling clay piece. Tap the mold gently to allow air bubbles to rise to the surface.

= Plaster Casting

Step 16—Allow the newly poured plaster to harden. Refer to the drying directions on the plaster of paris packaging to find out how much time to allow. (Most plaster of paris hardens in 30 to 45 minutes.) Then gently remove your plaster fruit.

Step 17—Use a rasp to file away the pour plug, and allow your plaster fruit to dry thoroughly. This might take several days.

Step 18—When your plaster fruit is dry, you can paint it with acrylic paints.

SCULPTURE 37

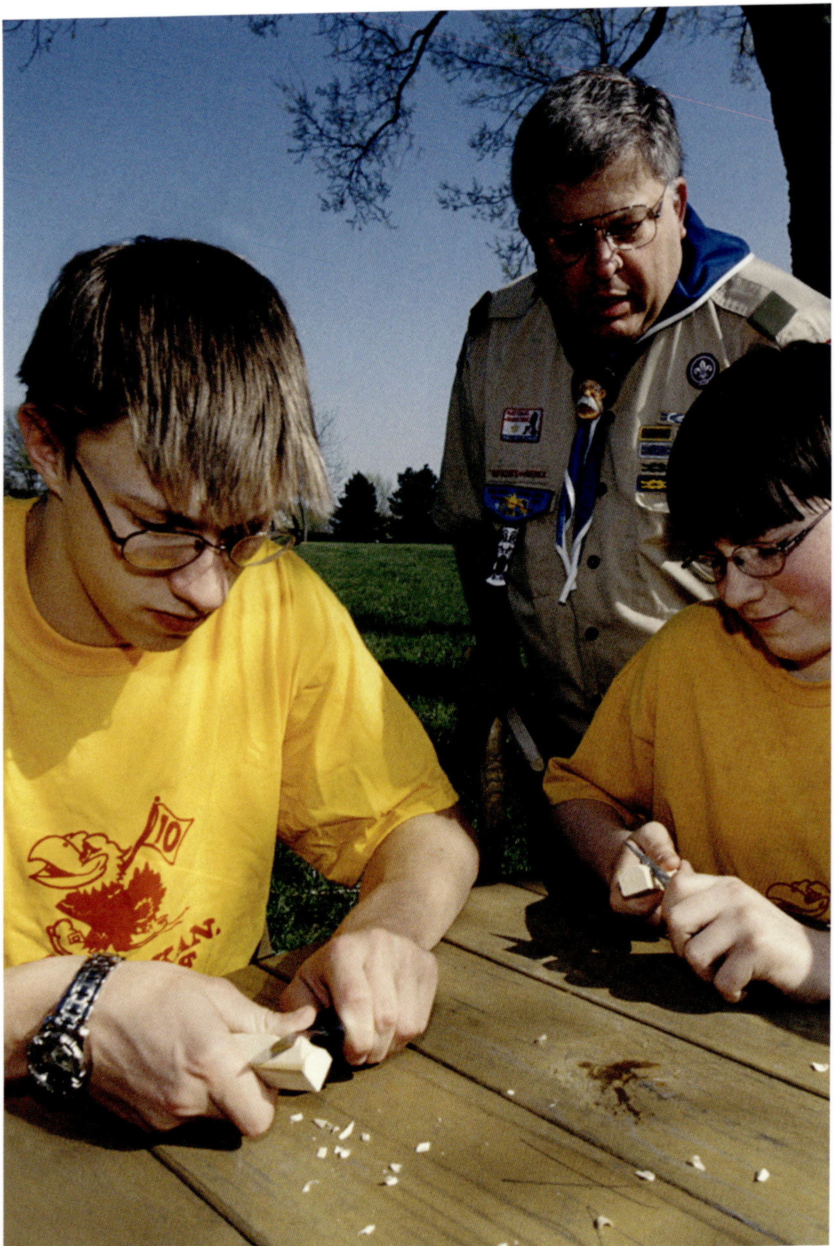
10

Carving in Wood

You will be most successful in fulfilling the requirement to sculpt a person or animal out of wood if you choose a soft wood, such as *balsa wood* or pine. These woods are relatively easy to carve. Start by drawing an outline of the image you want to shape on the block of wood. The piece of wood has six sides, so you will have to draw your image from the front, back, right and left sides, and top and bottom.

To be safe, carve away from your body. Make sure your tools are sharp—dull tools make wood carving dangerous. If a piece is difficult to cut, you might be trying to carve through too much wood at one time, or your knife blade might be dull.

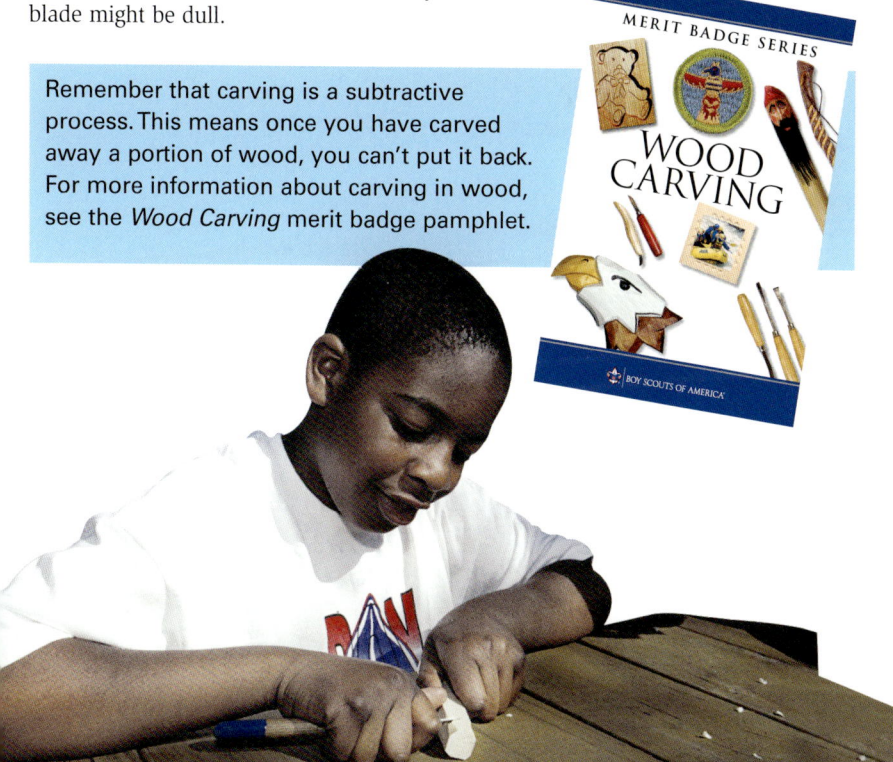

Remember that carving is a subtractive process. This means once you have carved away a portion of wood, you can't put it back. For more information about carving in wood, see the *Wood Carving* merit badge pamphlet.

CARVING IN WOOD

Carve Carefully

Remember to

- Always carve away from your body and keep your fingers out of the path of the knife's blade.
- Always take your time when using sharp tools. Never rush carving.
- Keep your work well away from your face, and never carve on your lap.
- Always carve on a clean and stable work surface and use a sturdy chair.
- Make small, well-placed carving strokes rather than long strokes.
- Always keep knives in a safe place, away from children.

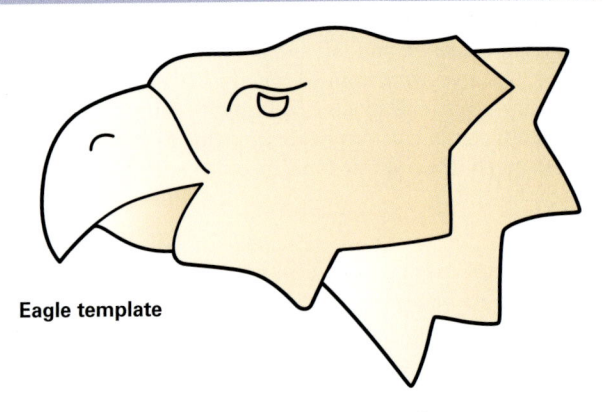

Eagle template

The Eagle Neckerchief Slide©*

This simple wood carving makes a good project for new wood carvers. To make the slide you will need the following supplies.

☐ Wood

☐ Wood-carving tools

☐ ½-inch or ¾-inch diameter PVC pipe cut into a 1-inch length

☐ Instant glue or epoxy

☐ Acrylic paints

☐ Assorted small paintbrushes

*This plan for the eagle neckerchief slide is the property of Jeff Springer, Topeka, Kansas, and is reproduced here with his permission.

CARVING IN WOOD

Step 1—Transfer the eagle design onto a block of wood that measures 3 3/8 inches with the grain and 2 1/4 inches across the grain. Use basswood, if possible.

Step 2—Cut or carve away the outside profile of the eagle.

Step 3—Score the line separating the beak and the top part of the eagle's head. Then, carve back to your score line, keeping the beak flat for the time being.

Step 4—Score the line separating the upper and lower parts of the beak. Carve the lower part of the beak so that it is recessed from the top. Next, round off and shape the top of the beak.

Step 5—Score the back part of the eagle's head. Carve back and use a stop cut to the line that you have scored. Slightly round off the top and bottom of this back portion of the head.

Step 6—Slightly carve the top, bottom, and edges of the main part of the eagle's head. To add more definition to the eagle's features, carve a little bit of wood off where the back of the head meets the neck and where the front of the head meets the beak.

Step 7—Carve the eye and nostril.

Step 8—In a well-ventilated space, glue the PVC ring to the back of the carving. Let the glue dry thoroughly and paint the slide. The eagle in the slide shown has a yellow beak, a white head, and a brown neck. The eye and nostril are black.

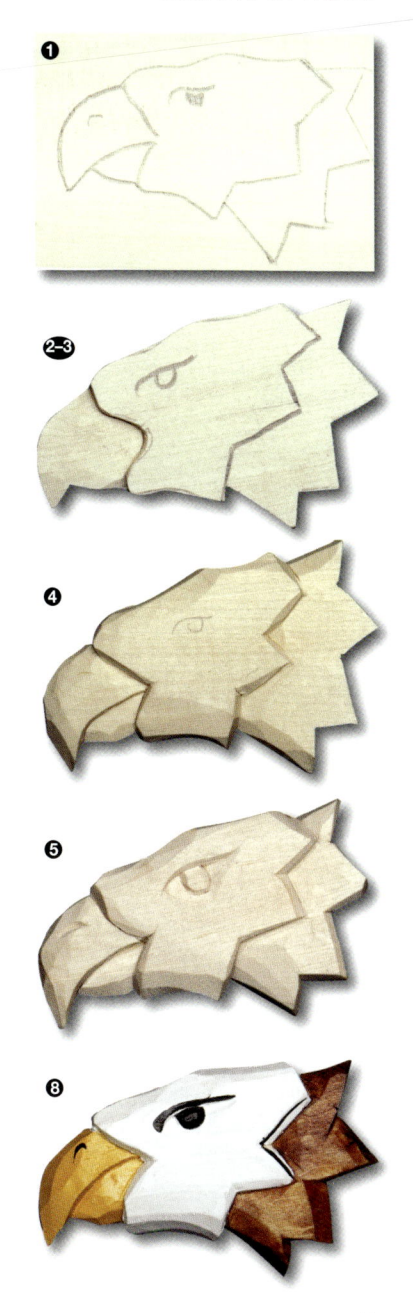

SCULPTURE 41

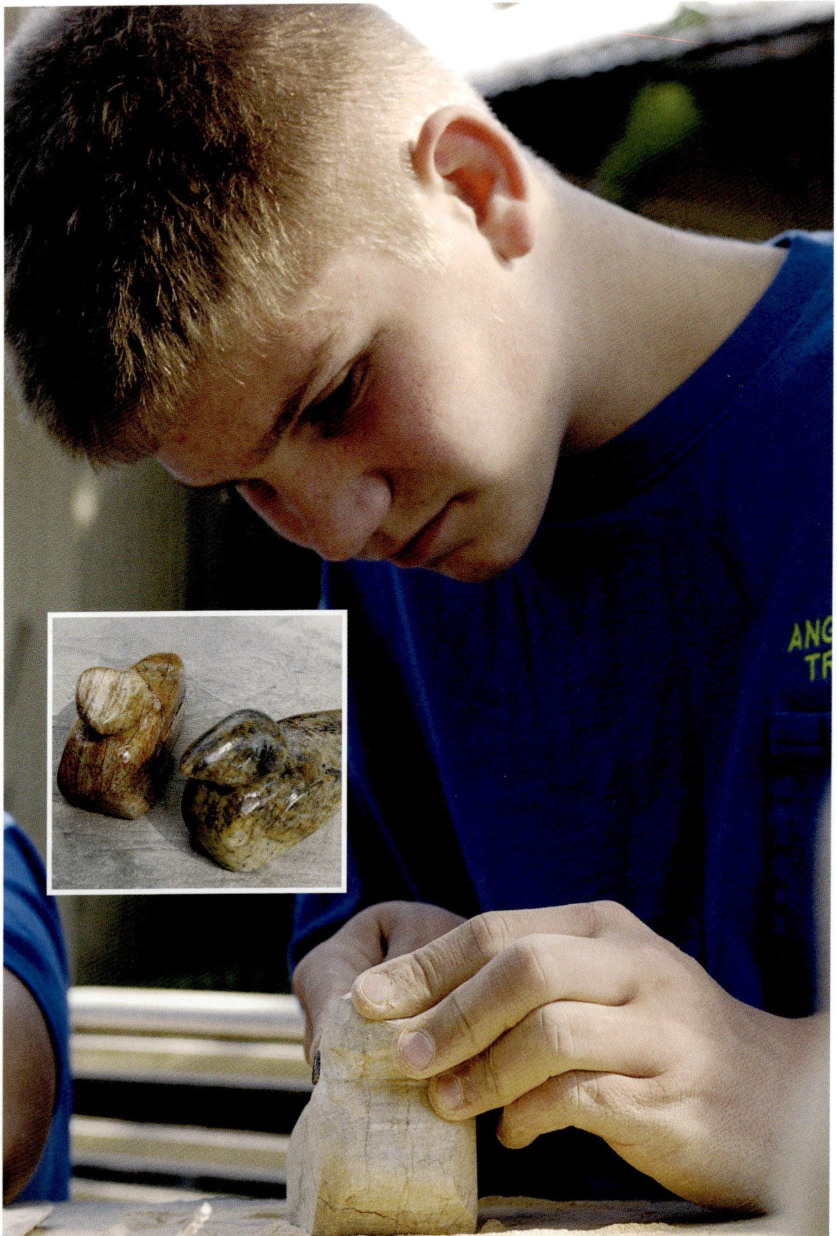

CARVING IN SOAPSTONE

Carving in Soapstone

Soapstone is a soft rock that has been popular with carvers for centuries. It comes in a variety of colors and, true to its name, has a slippery, soapy feel. Carving is a subtractive process, so when working with soapstone you must have an idea of what the finished form should look like before you start. A sketch on paper or a clay model the same size as the sculpture can serve as a guide.

TUNG OIL

COMBINATION RASP
RIFFLER
RASP

SANDPAPER

HACKSAWS

The following tools are useful for working with soapstone.

- Rasp—Similar to a file, but with large teeth on its surface.
- Riffler—A file or rasp that is curved or double-ended with different scraping shapes. Use it on concave surfaces and for hard-to-reach areas.
- Combination rasp—A combination tool with a flat file on one side and a half-rounded rasp on the other.
- Hacksaw—A handsaw with small teeth on a metal blade stretched taut across a frame.
- Minihacksaw—A smaller version of the hacksaw.
- Wet sandpaper—Specially treated sandpaper that is used to smooth file marks off of soapstone.
- Tung oil or boiled linseed oil—Oils that are used as quick-drying finishers.

Carving tools are sharp. To avoid injury, always saw or file away from your body. Remember also to wear safety glasses and a respiratory mask to avoid breathing in particles.

SCULPTURE 43

CARVING IN SOAPSTONE

Removing excess stone is a slow process and should not be hurried because the stone is soft and will break. Plus, once the material is removed, there is no way to replace it or add it back.

To carve a mourning dove, you will need a block of soapstone that is approximately 5 by 5 by 3 inches. You won't have to remove much excess stone, so you can just use a wood rasp and a riffle to carve the sculpture. If you were working on a larger, more advanced piece, you might use a hacksaw and a variety of chisels.

> You can find most of the supplies you will need at a local crafts store. You can also order supplies and kits over the internet (with your parent's permission and help). Be sure the soapstone you buy is labeled as nontoxic.

Step 1—Using heavy paper, make a scaled side-view drawing of the mourning dove. If you use a scale of 1 inch equals 3 inches, you will carve a bird that is 4 inches long—in proportion to a real-life mourning dove.

Step 2—Make a template by cutting out the drawing.

Step 3—Study the soapstone and decide which faces of the stone will be the right side, left side, top, bottom, front, and back of the sculpture. Use a pencil or wax pen to trace the outline of the template on the correct face of the soapstone. Lines can be redrawn or adjusted as you go.

> Before carving, use a pencil or wax pen to trace your template onto both sides of the block of soapstone.

Step 4—Block the piece by cutting away the larger unnecessary pieces of soapstone with a saw. Be careful not to cut too far—once stone is cut off, it's gone!

Step 5—With a rasp, rough out the side design by filling from the top of the stone down to the upper line of the wings. File in a forward motion only (away from your body). Be careful not to file areas already outlined.

Step 6—Following the template, continue to remove excess stone. You will want to leave a flat area on the bottom side as a base for the dove. Do not work too long on any one side. This is a three-dimensional piece, so move the stone around to view it from all angles as you work. This will help you create a balanced sculpture. Little by little, the mourning dove will start to emerge.

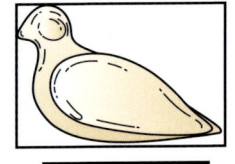

Do not use an ink or felt-tip pen; soapstone is so porous that the ink will bleed into the stone.

---

44   SCULPTURE

CARVING IN SOAPSTONE

Step 7—When you get close to the design lines, use a riffler to complete the shape of the bird and carve the fine details.

Step 8—The texture of the final surface is up to you. You can leave the file marks showing, or you can use sandpaper to polish it to a shine. To begin polishing the sculpture, smooth the surface with 150-grit sandpaper. Continue sanding with progressively finer sandpaper until the piece is as smooth as you want it to be. If you want your piece to be very smooth and shiny, finish polishing with 0000 grade steel wool.

Step 9—Use a soft cloth to dust your piece of any fine particles. If you want your mourning dove to have a shiny surface, cover the piece with a light coat of tung oil or boiled linseed oil. Wipe off any excess oil and allow the stone to sit overnight before you add another coat. Let the surface dry, then buff the sculpture with a soft cloth.

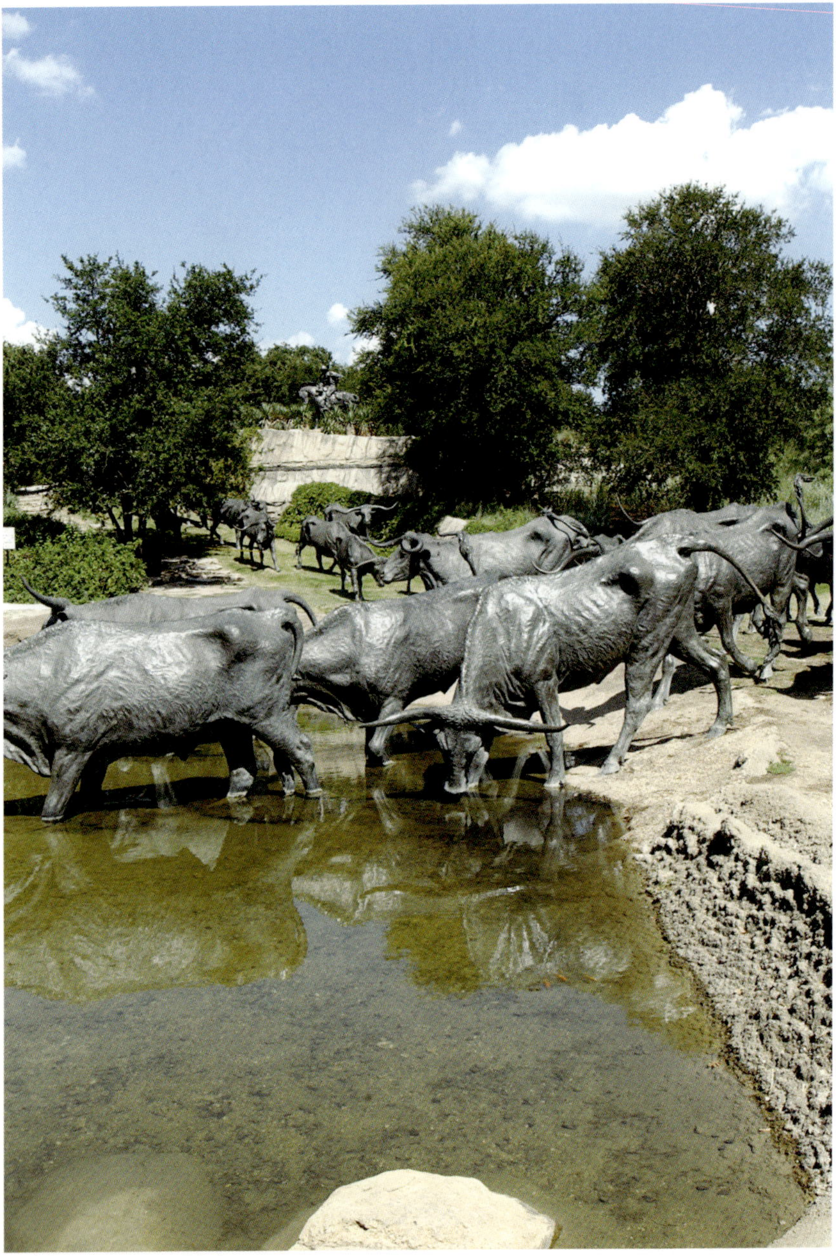

= Experimenting With Sculpture

Experimenting With Sculpture

There are many ways to explore the possibilities for making sculpture. In the world of art, there are no single solutions; any rules can be challenged. Artists have always experimented with what is available, looking for new ways to use the materials.

Find new and different ideas about what to make in books and on the internet (with your parent's permission). Many sculptors find inspiration in "found" objects, things people discard as junk—broken furniture, machine parts, light fixtures, and so forth.

SCULPTURE 47

Experimenting With Sculpture

Making a Mobile

To make a simple mobile that moves and changes constantly with air currents, you will need the following.

☐ Pen or pencil

☐ White or colored poster paper

☐ Scissors

☐ Wooden dowel, 10 inches long and 1/8 inch in diameter

☐ Cotton string of any color

☐ Acrylic paint

☐ Paintbrushes

☐ Ruler

☐ Cup hook

☐ White glue

48   SCULPTURE

Experimenting With Sculpture

Step 1—Draw the shapes of four realistic or abstract objects on the poster paper. You can make all four shapes identical or you can make them all different. Each shape should be about 3 inches by 4 inches. Cut out the shapes and paint them as desired.

Step 2—Find a place to suspend the mobile. Tie a 3-foot-long piece of string from one end of the dowel to the other. Tie another piece of string to the center of the 3-foot string. Make the string the length you will need in order to suspend your mobile from your selected spot.

Step 3—Glue one end of a piece of string to each of your paper objects, then loop the other end of the string around the dowel and tie a knot to secure each object. Suspend the paper objects at varying lengths from the dowel. The first object should be tied so that it hangs about $5\frac{1}{2}$ inches from the dowel; another should be at $1\frac{3}{4}$ inches; another at $5\frac{3}{4}$ inches; and the other at $2\frac{1}{8}$ inches.

Step 4—Screw a cup hook into the spot where you want to suspend the mobile. Tie the hook to the center string, or tape or tack the string in place instead of using a cup hook.

Step 5—After you suspend your mobile, adjust the positions of the objects on the dowel until they are balanced and moving without bumping into each other.

Sculpting in Ice

Some sculptures are made of materials that have been around for thousands of years, such as marble, bronze, and clay. Other sculptures last for only a few hours. Some sculptors create their short-lived works of art from blocks of ice.

Ice blocks are made from pure water, distilled or filtered to remove all chemicals and impurities. The companies that make ice used by ice sculptors have developed their own techniques for handling and freezing the water to minimize air bubbles, fractures, and other flaws in the ice blocks, and to increase the clarity of the ice.

Ice sculptors often have to wear protective clothing to avoid getting ice burns from being in constant contact with ice.

SCULPTURE 49

Experimenting With Sculpture

Ice sculptures vary in size, from small figurines to huge pieces weighing as much as several tons. These large pieces are made from several blocks of ice fused together with heat. The artist uses a chainsaw to form the basic shape of the object and then uses chisels and handsaws to carve the details. Sometimes the sculptor polishes the ice with heating elements or illuminates the piece with colored lights.

There is almost no limit to what can be sculpted from ice. On ocean cruises, passengers often get to watch artists create ice sculptures of subjects such as fish, castles, and carousels. People do not expect ice sculptures to last. Part of appreciating the beauty of an ice sculpture is watching it undergo interesting changes as it melts.

Experimenting With Sculpture

Four sand sculptors from Team Sandtastic, Sarasota, Florida, took less than a week to sculpt this medieval castle. Team Sandtastic offers these tips for sculpting in sand.

- Cut out the inside bottom rim of a 5-gallon bucket for a quick, inexpensive mold.
- Use a 2-foot section of a 2-by-4 as a tamper to solidify the structure.
- Use cement-working tools (spreaders, margin trowels) to form the sand. Other handy tools include shovels, D-handle spades, and small paintbrushes.
- Add detail with tools from the kitchen, such as spatulas, melon ball scoops, straws, measuring spoons, cake icing spreaders, and wooden skewers. Be sure to ask your parent for permission before using any household tools.

Place the bucket upside-down where you want your sculpture. Start packing wet (not soupy or dry) sand inside the bucket, 3 inches at a time. After packing each layer, tamp straight down with the 2-by-4. Keep the bucket straight, and always tamp straight down. Continue adding sand, packing, and tamping until you reach the top of the bucket. Then firmly tap the sides of the bucket and remove it by pulling up from the bottom (never from the top) of the bucket. You now have a block to start carving your sculpture.

Start with the largest tools to "block out" the basic shape of your design. Don't be afraid to move the sand around; you can always add and build on by using the bucket. For a more exciting design, consider creating a theme rather than just building a figure.

Delivering this 28-foot-high sculpture to the installation site required a crane, cherry picker, and flatbed truck. Sculptor Jean Woodham's studio in Westport, Connecticut, stands 40 feet high.

Art Spaces and Places

Making art is—generally—a solitary effort. Most sculptors and other fine artists work alone in private spaces or studios. Every work space is different. Some sculptors create small-scale pieces in a studio in their homes. Others create large-scale sculptures. Because they may work with toxic or flammable materials and dangerous equipment, they often work in studios fitted with exhaust systems, hoists, and rigs.

Try to arrange a visit to a sculptor's studio. Notice which materials and special equipment the artist uses. You might ask the artist why he or she decided to become a sculptor. Find out how the sculptor uses art for self-expression and for communicating with others.

Art Speaks

Art is a visual language that speaks for the artist and to the viewer. First, art is a means of self-expression, a way for the artist to create something tangible out of his or her emotions and ideas. Through the act of creating shapes, forms, and images, artists clarify their beliefs and personal theories. The final piece of artwork—no matter how chaotic it may appear—is an organized arrangement of design elements that represents the artist's point of view.

Second, art provokes a reaction from the viewer. You may look at a piece of art and think, WOW!—or walk away from it shaking your head in confusion. Or it may make you sad or angry.

Western Tori I: Sungate, a welded bronze and brass sculpture by Jean Woodham

Art Spaces and Places

One goal of the visual arts—particularly the fine arts (sculpture, painting, photography, and printmaking)—is to improve the world by getting people to think differently about it. An important value of looking at art is recognizing something about yourself by analyzing the way you react to the artwork. You become more socially tolerant, culturally sensitive, and even compassionate when you slow down and question whether you prejudged the art. Did you reject the piece because the subject matter offended you or because the people and setting were from a culture other than your own? Did you take the time to consider what the artist was trying to communicate to you?

Sometimes artists want to shock you. They may create works that reveal prejudice, hatred, violence, or hunger. They want viewers to realize that people in the world need help. The art might then prompt viewers to think about what they could do to help resolve these problems. In a way, art speaks for those who cannot speak for themselves.

Exhibiting Art

Some artists create art for their own enjoyment. They are not concerned about whether other people see their work or if anyone buys a piece. Most sculptors, however, want to build a reputation as an artist and to sell their work. They know that in order to achieve those goals, they will have to exhibit their work so that others may see what they have created.

Artists may join a co-op gallery in which the artist-members pay for and operate the gallery. The focus of the co-op is to get exposure—to present the artists' work to the art world and to the interested public. Few artists sell enough work in a co-op to support themselves, but often an art dealer may "discover" artists there and invite them to show their art in commercial galleries.

A commercial gallery is in business to sell art. A gallery owner or art dealer offers to represent an artist (along with others) and agrees to give the artist a solo show once every year or two. Because the gallery markets the artist's work and sets up the exhibitions, the gallery keeps between 40 and 60 percent of the sales price. That seems like a lot, but the commercial gallery attracts a larger, more serious audience than a co-op. Other dealers come, as do important art collectors and art critics who review the artist's work in newspapers and magazines. A good review helps generate attention and sales, and helps build an artist's reputation.

Artists who have made a name for themselves might have their work purchased by a museum. A museum houses and makes available rare, valuable, and famous art for the public to enjoy. The artwork is not for sale. It might have been purchased or donated, or it might be on loan from private collections or from other museums. If an artist achieves a significant reputation, a museum might show his or her work in a solo exhibition or combined with other artists.

If you choose to visit a museum, art gallery, artists' co-op, or art exhibit, approach the experience from several points of view: as the artist showing the work, as the viewer, and as the gallery owner or museum director. You will discover that many people and many decisions are involved in making, showing, and selling art.

ART SPACES AND PLACES

> ## Touch This!
> Some sculptors actually want people to interact with their works of art by encouraging them to touch, feel—even use—the sculpture.

Black Slide Mantra

***Black Slide Mantra,* Sapporo, Hokkaido, Japan.** Sculptor Isamu Noguchi (1904–1988) created this slide for a park. It was carved in black stone so that the sculpture could be seen even during the snowy winters of Sapporo. Noguchi wanted the piece to cultivate a sense of imaginative play in children. The spiral structure consists of a short staircase in back that leads to the slide at the top. Noguchi once said, "The completion of this sculpture will be when children polish it with their bottoms as they slide down." The slide was completed after his death, and children today continue to slide down the *Black Slide Mantra*, polishing the black stone along the way.

***Civil Rights Memorial,* Montgomery, Alabama.** Sculptor and architect Maya Lin (1959–) wanted the memorial to remind people about all the principal players and events of the Civil Rights movement. She accomplished this by creating a "water table," a circular fountain engraved with a time line of the movement. Visitors can run their fingers across the thin layer of water that flows over the water table, and they can touch the names and events inscribed in the black granite. The concept

ART SPACES AND PLACES

Civil Rights Memorial, **by Maya Lin**

came to her when she read Martin Luther King Jr.'s "I Have a Dream" speech, which rephrases a passage from the Bible: "No, no, we are not satisfied, and we will not be satisfied *until justice rolls down like waters and righteousness like a mighty stream."* Lin used a wall of granite, inscribed with those words, as a backdrop for the water table.

Face the Jury, St. Petersburg, Florida.

When Douglas Kornfeld's collection of chairs was being installed at the St. Petersburg Judicial Center, he said, "I hope people climb all over them." The chairs are meant to represent the participatory aspect of the jury system. There are 12 "juror" chairs, each one oversized and diverse in shape to represent the diversity of a jury. Most of the chairs stand around 6 feet high but seem even taller atop their posts, mounds of dirt and grass that elevate some chairs to as high as 10 feet. The 13th chair, of ordinary proportion, sits at ground level, facing the "jury" and representing the defendant.

Douglas Kornfeld's *Face the Jury*

SCULPTURE 57

Careers in Sculpture

As you have already learned from reading the previous chapter, many people are interested in sculpture—whether they want to make it, sell it, show it, or buy it. Fine artists feel a personal drive to make art, so they will often try to make a full-time career of it. Some sculptors have creative talent as well as a head for business and perhaps a flair for self-promotion, but others need help getting their artwork shown and sold.

A sculptor—like every self-employed artist—must be self-motivated and self-disciplined. No one else is going to make you go to work or finish a project. If you make large artwork that takes a long time to complete, you will have to be able to keep up your interest in the work. And if your work is a commissioned piece—that is, if someone hires you to create a piece—you will have to deliver the piece to the buyer by the agreed-upon deadline.

Most self-employed sculptors have a difficult time supporting themselves strictly from the sale of their pieces. They usually have to supplement their income through related opportunities such as teaching sculpture in colleges or in workshops.

Some people choose careers, such as those listed below, in which they can be involved with art and sculpture without actually creating it.

- If you think you would enjoy helping another artist create a large-scale sculpture, then you might be interested in a career as a foundry worker or mold maker.

- If you have a talent for selling things, you might enjoy a career as an artist's agent, art appraiser, art auctioneer, art consultant, art dealer, or gallery owner.

- If you like art history, you might consider a career as an art historian, art librarian, museum curator, conservator, or restorer.

CAREERS IN SCULPTURE

- If you like to write, you might enjoy a career as an art writer, art critic, or art reviewer.
- If you enjoy teaching others, you might be interested in a career as an artist-in-residence, art teacher, museum educator, or workshop instructor.

Education and Training

If you want to pursue a career as a professional sculptor, you will need some studio lessons and hands-on training. You can start by finding out if your high school offers shop classes that will introduce you to the techniques for working with metal, wood, and plastics. Later, you can get hands-on training by working for another artist as an apprentice or assistant. If you intend to supplement your income in a related field, you might have to earn advanced degrees.

Colleges and universities offer four- and five-year programs that lead to bachelor of fine arts (BFA) or master of fine arts (MFA) degrees. Beyond the core courses common to all major areas of study, these programs include art history and studio art classes.

Independent schools of art and design offer two-year programs that lead to an associate of arts or bachelor of fine arts degree. These programs emphasize studio work.

Anyone who wants to teach art in public schools must have a bachelor's degree; you might also need a teaching certificate. For a permanent or full-time teaching position at the college level, you will need to earn a master of fine arts degree.

To find out more about specific careers related to sculpture or fine arts, refer to the resources section. Talk to your guidance counselor at school about the training and education requirements for those careers that interest you.

SCULPTURE 59

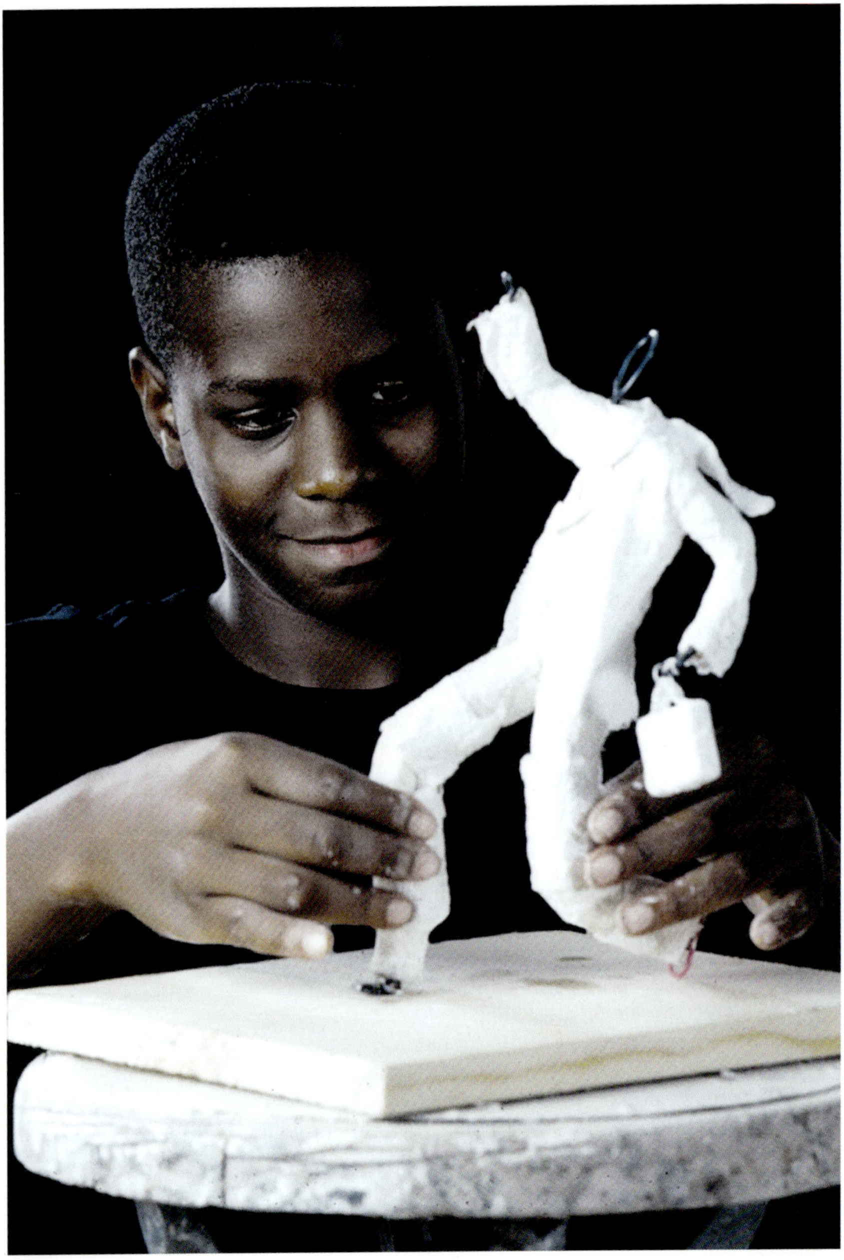

Sculpture Resources

By reading about the fine arts and art history, you can learn about sculpture dating from ancient times to the present. You might like to find out more about famous sculptors of the Renaissance such as Michelangelo, Donatello, and Cellini or more contemporary sculptors such as Auguste Rodin, Constantin Brancusi, Barbara Hepworth, Augustus Saint-Gaudens, Alberto Giacometti, Henry Moore, George Segal, and Alexander Calder. You also can find interviews with important contemporary sculptors, articles about the artists, and photographs of their work.

Artist Felix de Weldon sculpted this world-famous *U.S. Marine Corps War Memorial,* which is displayed in Arlington, Virginia. The memorial depicts the raising of the American flag at Iwo Jima, Japan. A cloth flag hangs from the 60-foot bronze flagpole. The bronze figures stand 32 feet tall.

Sculpture Resources

Scouting Literature

Architecture, *Art*, *Basketry*, *Graphic Arts*, *Leatherwork*, *Metalwork*, *Photography*, *Pottery*, and *Wood Carving* merit badge pamphlets

> With your parent's permission, visit the Boy Scouts of America's official retail website, www.scoutshop.org, for a complete listing of all merit badge pamphlets and other helpful Scouting materials and supplies.

Books

Barrie, Bruner Felton. *A Sculptor's Guide to Tools and Materials*, 2nd. ed. ABFS Publishing, 2007.

———. *Mold Making, Casting, and Patina for the Student Sculptor*. ABFS Publishing, 2000.

Brommer, Gerald F., and Joseph A. Gatto. *Careers in Art: An Illustrated Guide*. Davis Publications Inc., 1999.

Brown, Claire Waite, ed. *The Sculpting Techniques Bible: An Essential Illustrated Reference for Both Beginner and Experienced Sculptors*. Chartwell Books, 2006.

Carlson, Maureen. *How to Make Clay Characters*. North Light Books, 1997.

Camenson, Blythe. *Great Jobs for Art Majors*. McGraw-Hill, 2003.

Dewey, Katherine. *Creating Lifelike Figures in Polymer Clay: Tools and Techniques for Sculpting Realistic Figures*. Potter Craft, 2008.

Erdmann, Dottie. *Hands On Sculpting*. Columbine Communications & Publications, 1992.

Friesen, Christi. *Steampunkery: Polymer Clay and Mixed Media Projects*. CF Books, 2010.

Hessenberg, Karin. *Sculpting Basics: Everything You Need to Know to Create Three-Dimensional Artworks*. Barron's Educational Series, 2005.

Lanteri, Edouard. *Modelling and Sculpting Animals*. Dover Publications, 1985.

———. *Modelling and Sculpting the Human Figure*. Dover Publications, 1985.

Lark Books. *The Figure in Clay: Contemporary Sculpting Techniques by Master Artists*. Lark Crafts, 2005.

Lucchesi, Bruno, and Margit Malmstrom, contributor. *Modeling the Head in Clay*. Watson-Guptill Publications, 1996.

Miller, Richard M. *Figure Sculpture in Wax and Plaster*. Dover Publications, 1987.

Plowman, John. *The Sculptor's Bible: The All-Media Reference to Surface Effects and How to Achieve Them*. Krause Publications, 2005.

Reynolds, Donald Martin. *Masters of American Sculpture: The Figurative Tradition From the American Renaissance to the Millennium*. Abbeville Press, 1994.

Rich, Jack C. *The Materials and Methods of Sculpture*. Dover Publications, 1988.

Salmon, Mark. *Opportunities in Visual Arts Careers*. McGraw-Hill, 2008.

Slobodkin, Louis. *Sculpture: Principles and Practice*. Dover Publications, 1973.

Teixidó i Camí, Josepmaria, and Jacinto Chicharro Santamera. *Sculpture in Stone*. Barron's Educational Series, 2001.

Sculpture Resources

Periodicals

Sculpture
Telephone: 609-689-1051
Website: www.sculpture.org

Sculpture Review
Telephone: 212-764-5645
Website:
https://sculpturereview.com

Organizations and Websites

The Art Career Project
Website:
www.theartcareerproject.com

International Sculpture Center
14 Fairgrounds Road, Suite B
Hamilton, NJ 08619-3447
Telephone: 609-689-1051
Website: www.sculpture.org

National Sculptors' Guild
Telephone: 970-667-2015
Website:
www.nationalsculptorsguild.com

National Sculpture Society
Website:
https://nationalsculpture.org

Acknowledgments

The Boy Scouts of America is grateful to Jean Woodham for providing images of her sculpture and her studio in Westport, Connecticut, and to her daughter, Melissa Deur, for securing the images on behalf of the BSA.

The Boy Scouts of America is grateful to the men and women serving on the National Merit Badge Subcommittee for the improvements made in updating this pamphlet.

We appreciate Lynn Bartlett, Sierra Hills Stone (sierrahillsstone.com), Angels Camp, California, for her assistance with photography.

Jean Woodham has been creating abstract sculpture for more than six decades. She was one of the first artists to use welding and industrial applications to create large-scale outdoor sculptures.

Jean Woodham has exhibited her work in group shows with David Smith, Louise Nevelson, and other well-known sculptors. She has shown her sculpture in a large artists' co-op, in galleries, and in museums around the world. More than 150 of her sculptures are in private and public collections, including installations for the NS *Savannah* (the first nuclear-powered merchant ship), the World Bank, headquarters of major companies, and university campuses.

Jean Woodham, sculptor

SCULPTURE RESOURCES

Photo and Illustration Credits

Crazy Horse Memorial, Crazy Horse, South Dakota, courtesy—pages 6 (*Korczak Ziolkowski*) and 7 (*overhead view*)

The Gihon Foundation, courtesy—page 10

Douglas Kornfeld, courtesy—page 57 (*Face the Jury photos*)

Shutterstock.com—cover (*tiger*, ©GOLFX; *colorful clay figurine*, ©Zerbor); pages 6 (*Mount Rushmore*, ©Guy J. Sagi), 12 (*©Refat*), 14 (*clay*, ©Beykov Maksim; *blocks*, ©BOULENGER Xavier; *welder*, ©Dusan Petkovic; *sculpture of face*, ©Kateryna Omelianchenko), 15 (*lattice*, ©Robyn Mackenzie), 16 (*mobile*, ©woraatep suppavas), 27 (©stoatphoto), 33 (©Kozlik), 47 (*metal flower*, ©Andrei Sikorskii), 48 (*palette*, ©Lotus_studio), 49 (©Ann Bulashen...

ice tow...
(©Ant...
59 (©...

©Jeff Spri...
courte...

Teamsandtastic.com, courtesy—page 51

Three Soldiers ©1984, Hart & VVMF—page 8

Wikipedia.org, courtesy—pages 3, 7 (*color image*), 9, 11, and 57 (*Civil Rights Memorial*)

Wikipedia and Wikimedia Commons image from used Chris 73, courtesy, freely available at http://commons.wikimedia.org/wiki/Image:MoguchiBlackSlideMantraOutside.jpg under the creative commons cc0by-sa 2.5 license—page 56 (*both*)

Jean Woodham, courtesy—pages 4–5 (*both*), 52–53 (*both*), and 63

All other photos and illustrations not mentioned above are the property of or are protected by the Boy Scouts of America.

Dan Bryant—page 21

John McDearmon—illustrations on pages 13, 44, and 45

...*ting tools*, ...; pages 15 ...*ools*), ...*re*), 25–26 ...*(all)*, 48 ...60

64